The Eucalypt Distillery

Also by Michele Fermanis-Winward & published by Ginninderra Press
Threading Raindrops
To the Dam (Pocket Poets)
The Sail Weaver (Pocket Poets)

Michele Fermanis-Winward

The Eucalypt Distillery

Acknowledgements

Previous versions of some poems have appeared in:
Mountains: oblique angles
Celebrating Life
Aleola
Trainstorm
Silver Birch Press
Red Room Company: The Disappearing
and *First Refuge* (Ginninderra Press).

Thanks are due to The Siding Writers:
Vanessa Kirkpatrick, Emma Brazil, Brendan Doyle
Tom Williams, John Lekkas and Craig Billingham.
My love and gratitude to the group for guiding
many of the poems in this collection.

Particular thanks are due to Brendan Doyle
and my husband Kevin for their sensitive editing.

I dedicate this collection to Deb Westbury
who showed me it was possible.

The Eucalypt Distillery
ISBN 978 1 76041 469 6
Copyright © text Michele Fermanis-Winward 2017
Cover image: Marie Therese Elz

First published 2017 by
GINNINDERRA PRESS
PO Box 3461 Port Adelaide 5015 Australia
www.ginninderrapress.com.au

Contents

Summer	7
The Word is Beautiful	9
The Runaway	10
Galahs	11
Passing By	12
Reading the Lines	13
Breathing Out	14
Landfall	15
The Tribe	16
Crossing by Seashell	17
Blackberries	18
In Place	19
Storm Dogs	20
Disturbed	21
No Ending	22
A is for Arid	23
From Above	25
Autumn	27
Primitive	29
White Water Rush	30
Wasted	31
Nightjar	32
The Tramp	33
Grevillea	34
Among the Apple Trees	35
From the maze	36
On the edge	37
Ironstone Mountain	38
At Motel Topiary	39
Approaching Winter	40
We Descend	41
The Journey Home	42

Winter — 43

- Blue — 45
- The Geologist — 46
- Bypassed — 47
- Growth Rings — 48
- Wild — 49
- The Walking Classroom — 50
- Seeing — 51
- The Eagle — 52
- The Old Cocky — 53
- The Black Wind — 54
- Soon — 55
- Taken — 56
- I am more — 57
- Heritage — 58

Spring — 59

- Wollemi — 61
- Off Track — 62
- Hunger — 63
- Ringtail — 64
- Natural Light — 65
- Until today — 66
- How to Make a Home — 67
- The Bowerbird — 68
- The Colony — 69
- The Work of Noise — 70
- Plovers in the Park — 71
- The Watchers — 72
- Shearwater — 73
- Fire Ready — 74
- Fire Healing — 75
- Devotional — 76

Summer

The Word is Beautiful

There are words, invisible threads
slung between branches,
they capture the changes,
whisper to the trees,
find shelter in pools of mist.

Wet leaves become light-brushes
for words to paint the shadows,
turn black and grey bright colour.

Words are feathers, ephemeral,
long spikes of green and blue,
the fragile reds and yellows,
they make unruly chatter,
gather in corners, swirl
on the wing-beats of summer.

Words unwrap their petals
offer complex perfume to the air,
blend notes of spice and fruit.

Down twisting paths I find
a word to guide my way,
the one to nourish life,
a word with power to heal,
the power to make me whole.

The Runaway

Beside the track
a meadow blooms,
sun sharp
with evening primrose,
dandelion,
the acid-yellow weeds.

Empty grass heads blow
ragged in the wind,
set their seeds
derelict, unmown,
against the heat and noise
of rattling iron.

Galahs

Their sound
cuts through the years.

Wheeling cries
above gnarled peppercorn,
one patch of shade
I drove all day to reach,
my camp beside a water bore,
galahs waiting for its overflow.

Stark against a turning sky,
concrete monoliths,
the silos ringed by sound,
massed feathers pink and grey
spun into sunset red.

Far west,
dark's plunge to cold
from dust and sweat,
of being on the wheat,
my nights of silent drink.

Galahs at dawn,
their noise
woke me to heat and thirst.

Passing By

Loose rolling hills
languid in the sun.
Among old stumps
granite knots
hunch lichen bound
weathering soft green.

The dusty bulk of sheep
grows indistinct
in tassel-headed grass,
new wool caked brown
from summer rain and mud.

We're driving
state to state
bypassing border towns,
their names
are signposts to the past.

Reading the Lines

We ridge a winding road
through dairy-fattened hills,
a vibrant green, close terracing,
two centuries of cattle hooves
balancing their weight of milk
are carved into the slope.

We drop to wetland sedge,
river flats give way to coast,
a coarse sand yellow beach,
we find pale fossil shells
trapped in baseline cliffs
of fretted shale with ironstone.

A laying down and oozing out
through millennial time,
the steady slap of waves
as tidal scour and flux reduce
these tracks of ancient life
down to a single line.

Breathing Out

The sound of water
is a thousand pebbles
tossed into the air,
a thwump of waves
against hard rock.
It's squashed between
the roar of footy club PAs.

From the park a band
is belting out its song.
I watch a currawong
passing overhead,
beat, beat and glide to rest,
beat, beat and glide again.

The beach on Sunday
smells of fish and chips,
hot oil with petrol fumes,
seaweed and brine.
A straggle line of walkers
heads to the point,
children urging parents,
others towed by dogs.

At the cliff a midday sun
meets ocean breeze
and the small knot
trapped inside my lungs
unwinds itself and breathes.

Landfall

I let the soft slap of waves ease over me,
their power is tempered by distance,
this drowsing bay of silt and tidal reach,
a shimmer of foam waking the horizon.

Far headlands catch the roar and burst of ocean
where hidden reefs and ragged shoals collide,
a nursery for gummy shark and seahorse
beyond the forest walls of kelp.

My toes curl against fragments of rust and
wormy wood, a green corroded button,
their stories held in archives – of men
and profits lost, claims of chance or blame.

At my feet the sea whispers of its storms,
here wrecks find sanctuary, the sailing ships
and steamers lost in pirate weather,
eaten by salt, their timber and iron slump,

they cling to sand and round the cliffs for home.

The Tribe

One small group
left Africa,
made their camps
led by the coast,
sharing all they owned.

Pushed by waves of men
with spear and club,
encroaching cold
and lack of food,
the tribe gained mastery
of its nomadic life.

They travelled south
into our furthest reach
until they found
a home to welcome them,
where man belonged to land.

Their lore was set
in lines of song,
the bonds of dance
and elemental dreams,
corroborees refreshed
the seasons of their feet.

When Earth no longer
fuels our needs
its fate is held in trust
by remnants of the tribe,
they can heal
what modern man corrupts.

Crossing by Seashell

Fat periwinkles in their brine,
green spirals filled with meat
to boil and needle from their shells.

I worked these rockpools as a child,
plastic bucket in my hand
when foraging was still allowed.

Once empty shells linked tribes,
they told a food was safe to eat
when others came this way.

The shore line now has changed,
their message dulled by time
deep within the layered clay.

Washed by storms from midden nests
and powdered in the sand,
lost to wind and sea.

Fat periwinkles in their brine,
green spirals filled with meat
to boil and needle from their shells.

The bridge I crossed millennia on.

Blackberries

Our slow way home from school,
we loved the reckless game
of fresh plucked, oozing fruit,
mouths and hands turned red.

We swatted flies,
spread the stain
across our sunburnt cheeks,
watched out for snakes
escaping from
the tangled web of thorns.

Bending in as far
as we could reach,
the prickles biting back
snagged our skin and clothes.

Imagined being trapped,
lost inside the core where
unknown shadows lived.
I do not see them now,
banned from farms,
the roadside ditch and path.

I can't recall their taste.

In Place

I am following a flattened path
of wombat tracks through long grass,
deep gouges lead to tunnels
with trellised entrance ways,
lichen-covered roots
exposed beneath dead trees.
I wake a mob of kangaroos
drowsing in the sun,
they melt to wattle scrub,
two fierce males stand tall,
set themselves on guard.

Moisture clings to shadows
late in the afternoon,
summer grass heads lift,
wind shivers through the leaves
and there is nowhere else to be.

Storm Dogs

Static
on the radio predicts the change
beyond what ears and eyes can note,
distorts the hourly list of accidents,
a politician's latest gaff and sport.

Wind
rattles doors, the sky turns sour,
leaves spin about the yard, I run,
harvest washing from the line before
another lightning shaft brings rain.

The dogs
begin to shake at growling overhead
as if a pack of wolves had their scent
and no escape was close,
my arms and lap chosen as defence,
but who will I cling to?

Disturbed

He stays
with a stillness
that is absolute
not coiled but warm
and loosely arabesqued
poised for flight
his lidless eyes are fixed
as I approach.

I have disturbed his work
the tongue-flick hunt
for mouse and frog
on circuits round the house
regret I do not see him
cross my path again
while he in perfect stillness
observes.

No Ending

Beached
on the high tide
of a summer afternoon
I stagnate,
slump on tousled sheets
that hold the shape
of last night's fitful hours.

No energy for pleasure or
desire to work, no thought
beyond myself.
I laze and fantasise.
Above the drone of air-con pump
a blackbird scrolls its melody
into the languid air,
my sultry day's ennui.

I wait, the hour strikes,
another news broadcast
of fires and loss, men pitched
to save a home or life
regardless of their own,
a war that never ends.

A is for Arid

i

She remembers
how the garden hummed
when she was lithe
and watched her forest rise
from seedling frail
into a shaded glen.

Bees purred all day,
birds filled her orchard
with their calls;
brief spikes to drawn out
rambling swirls.
Each daylight hour
had its choir and song.

Branches swept the ground
with fruit, parrots flocked;
red, blue and green,
picked flesh from drupes
to find young seeds
and chattered all the time.

At night soft acrobats
danced across her roof,
they swung from apple trees,
ate all the fruit
and then the leaves,
left telltale scats
and wisps of fur behind.

ii

Now all is sand
from years of drought
and winds that burnt,
her trees did not survive,
their fallen branches
powder at her touch,
replaced by mounds of rock.

She will not succumb
her hands grown stiff
with age and toil
she scoops a well,
plants cacti spurs,
fat green against dull brown,
her garden of the silent stones.

From Above

Braided remnants far below
arabesque through desert scrub,
leech black and russet brown,
shadows of lost riverways.

Ridges hung with veins of green,
their vast monotony bleeds out
until a homestead roof ignites
reflecting off the sun.

Outcrops weave ancient songs,
the spine and ribs of spirit time,
old bones left fingering the sand
dissolve from view at day's ebb.

Between myself and earth
clouds float, sharp pools of light
they turn, red as the distant land.

Autumn

Primitive

Bands of light are arrows to the ground
on shafts bright green or dark viridian.

The smell of earth, wood rot and fungi spores,
crushed ants beneath my feet.

This wilderness ensnares the primal
sensing brain, invokes an ancient DNA.

I'm charged by dancing particles of mist,
each step rewires the animist within.

Trees net spirits hunting in the clouds,
birds transpose our memories into song.

White Water Rush

Skidding over stones
an icy flush lifts moss,
churns gravel into sand,
it undermines creek banks.

Escarpments shed cascades,
scour crevices of ferns,
fell saplings brittle branches,
the roar of passing torrent.

A lyrebird takes fright
into the debris storm,
is swallowed by the foam
spun out of leaping water.

Wasted

Sunshine after rain
before the clouds return
scores an end to April
in storm-blown changing moods.

Thunder comes then hail,
it blasts leaves' tender veins,
snaps rows of white nerines,
the trees are bared to stems.

The ground is soft and green,
a sponge of wasted leaves
before the trees could draw
the sweetness they contained.

Nightjar

Rigid like a broken limb
on a curve of metal arch,
she's out of place against
buds of autumn rose,
her plumage is bark dun,
a cold-ash mottled grey.

Her mouth is opening to growl
when cockatoos screech past,
maintains her pose all day
except when we approach,
amber eyes and head rotate,
mind open to alarm.

With night, plump bush rats come,
drawn to a bin of seed,
they shimmy down the pipes,
feel a wind-beat thrust of wings,
meet the wide mouth snatch
and warmth of crushing dark.

The Tramp

He looks more hawk than cockatoo,
a head made small by lack of feathers,
blue skin without its crest of yellow.

Strong claws and powerful beak
that's aged to sharpened dagger,
a bald escutcheon on his breast.

He preens, flounces in the mist,
despite the state of shabby coat
this robust bird demands respect.

He feeds alone, is unperturbed
and battle scars give their rewards,
all other birds wait for him to leave.

Grevillea

Rails and mute cement,
the red brick walls
caged in cyclone wire's
hard-edged delineation.

Trucks drag their loads,
the coal train's grind,
dust wheezing out
clings to suburban grease,

tight fit of shops and flats
monotonous beneath
their layer of grime,
no frivolous distraction.

Until the shout
from one abandoned plot
that mutes all other sights,
native flowers, full blown

glow vibrant pink and gold.
They dance on acrid blasts
from speeding wheels
beside the rusting iron.

Among the Apple Trees

Here mist caresses
gnarled fingertips of trees,
their leaves are farewell notes
posted on the wind.

Trees whisper to the soil,
absorb its autumn lullaby
coaxing them to sleep,
remnant fruit decays
on a bed of amber sighs.

From the maze

of overwhelming noise,
traffic snarls and fumes
we climb,
unclench our teeth,
release tight chests,
no longer feel like
creatures in a pit.

We cross
the portal of dense mist,
reach our mountain home,
rug up against the cold
and give thanks
to live among
a silent wreath of clouds.

On the edge

I have become
a fringe dweller
in the country of my birth,
have no desire
for watching sport,
noisy chatter,
celebrity culture.

I want to
waste my time,
follow ribbons of ideas
picking at their tangles,
learn the secret
of belonging
on the earth,

to ride
bird-shaped
corridors of song,
curl inside their hollows,
feel bright wings
lift my dreaming hours,
unravel.

Ironstone Mountain

Blue light
folds into cloud,
becomes a turgid green,
our day suspends
as birdsong disappears.

We feel the strike,
windows shake
on thunder's pulse,
lightning shafts
drawn to metallic stone.

The ridge electrifies,
hairs stand erect,
a scent of ozone
replaces oil of eucalypt
in ionised, crackling air.

At Motel Topiary

native trees are
parodies of natural form,
small globes in tubs,
one square of close-cropped lawn
sulks behind a cube of hedge.

There is no dust or leaves,
the driveway has been scoured,
a line of sun glare seats
guard each door
with pots of sand for butts.

No small talk waiting here,
this tight ship
has a place for everything
with clear marked signs
for us recalcitrants.

We lumber in with all our mess,
fill the bins, leave greasy marks
on polished chrome and sink.
We scuff the carpet with our bags,
foul the air and leave.

Approaching Winter

The last maple leaves
spin like varnished bronze
in low-beam morning sun,
birds shuffle dirt for grubs.

My digging set aside,
time will compost drifts
of red and russet falls
piled high along the paths.

Possums eat rhubarb leaves
now the trees are bare,
ignore all native plants
and peel my citrus fruit.

I will buy them apples
to wedge in forks of trees,
I need lemons for myself
to fight the winter's cold.

We Descend

In the shade of sandstone cliffs,
narrow threading bitumen
curls through dusty sclerophyll
to reach the coachwood glen.

Before axe and bullock teams
tamed valley floor to sun, the wind
and crows, an ancient forest
spread its fingers south.

Moist air filtered by green light,
translucent tree ferns dense and still,
a wood-rot scented earth, where
boulders fell into the lap of moss.

This remnant clings to shadows
between high ridge and farms,
it speaks a tongue that's primitive
we translate deep inside.

The Journey Home

When I turn off internal noise
and eyelids close to dream
I feel what cells recall
beyond my sum of years.

I see wild ponies run the moors,
my nostrils flare as I inhale
a crush of herbs
beneath their dancing hooves.

I touch an ancient standing stone
in gorse fields at Land's End,
the fretted surface won't reveal
a faith it once proclaimed.

I hear the tramp of many feet
grind down a shingle road,
their path towards new lives
pledged to a distant land.

Breathing in all I have known,
the taste of salt from riding seas,
I hear a screeching cockatoo
it brings me home again.

Winter

Blue

The distance
is a promise
yet unknown
dissolving
into clouds
my breath
is mingling
with the air
once breathed
by men
who carved
their dreams
in stone.

The Geologist

A sideways glance
towards my love,
his eyes intent upon the road
as he reveals our country's depth
beneath the flow of bitumen.

His stories plot a map
of how the land was formed,
he pans a river in his mind
to list each mineral
broken from the ground.

Slab hut and mullock heap,
the lives of quarrymen,
prospectors after gold,
a seam I mine within his words
before the earth reclaims.

Bypassed

Grand hotels with shiny bars
no longer greet a lucky strike
or bumper crop, they doze,
wait for their lot to change.
Wide shops are empty caves,
window signs picked out in gold
now peel and fade to brown.

A charity store oozes stock,
cardboard boxes slumped outside
to catch a passer by,
hand knits' loose threads,
picked over scarves in nauseating beige,
a lilac vest that's pilled,
while beanies in the local footy's
green and white escape.

A few doors on the baker
with a love of cochineal
sells cakes and buns in lurid pink,
proclaims his town
'Home Of The Iced Gem Scone'.

Growth Rings

The years fold over us,
warmed by the breath of leaves,
the weight of sheltering limbs.

Together we were saplings
unsure if we could hold the ground,
weather storms and drought.

We spread our fragile threads
which strengthened into roots,
found paths through buried stone,

learnt trees adapt or fail
with time and climate change.
We looked beyond each loss,

mourned and from it grew,
reached towards the open sky
always striving for the light.

Wild

Wattlebird alarms,
defending claims
to sweetened cones
on coastal banksia scrub.
Sky and sea are cast in steel,
horizon's cutlass edge,
whale plumes rise
stark white against the clouds.

Yellow seed pods
strung along the sand,
rafts of wood and leaves
gouged from riverbanks
swept back to ride the shore.
Cunjevoi sweat, fat clumps
with bedrock still attached.

Fists of pumice hunch in groups,
deep sea magma blasts
snap frozen by the waves.
A frisbee waits to fly,
with shattered edge
it gamely limps away.

The Walking Classroom

Their names are clearly marked,
python tree and maiden's blush,
the drooping epiphytes, native ebony
and casuarina locked in vines.

The whoop and whistle of unseen birds,
fan palms spread among the ferns,
dense brown humus on the ground
a constant churn of life.

I step above the working soil
bouncing feet restrained by metal grids,
a serpentine elevated path
protecting lives beyond my gaze.

Buttressed trunks supporting distant crowns,
catbirds mewl like strangled wraiths,
a whipbird shapes its exclamation mark of sound
and school kids shout into the unbound sky.

Seeing

Through his eyes
a bowl becomes
cupped hands of clay
outstretched in offering.

The potter
bending to his work
hears a call
and lifts his gaze
to watch the bird
sweep past.

His hand
instinctive, following,
an upward stroke
from oxide-laden brush
is the beating wing
on a glaze of cobalt sky.

The Eagle

I live where sun first strikes the ridge,
rise as its warmth unknots my bones.
Wattles flower winter long,
turn muted greens a patchwork gold,
the valley fills with light,
I soar on pollen-scented air.

Early spring feeds serpent winds
that rock the home I built, like me
it frays, rubbed smooth with time,
my days are tightly bound,
held to the changing scarp.

Once mountain gums ringed my nest
and sheltered me from storms.
One by one, with years they fell
to fire and drought's decay,
each season's mark exposed
upon bald slabs of rock.

When morning gales are buffeting
I fold my head and nestle in.
Beyond the range of canyon walls
I ride on thermals of the mind
across new territories of dreams.

The Old Cocky

A shabby crest of sulphur yellow,
his feathers stained and ragged.
He is larger than the others,
young males who screech and swoop,
break the dawn and leave.

He shuffles down the path,
a broken beak now healed
sits askew his face,
with nimble claws
plies sunflower seeds to mouth.

We keep our dogs away,
he waits, observes, stays close,
spends the night by our back door
head tucked beneath his wing
until his strength returns.

The Black Wind

We tread along smooth tracks
fresh graded on our ridge,
the storm has changed it all,
a canopy once dense now sparse,
huge gums torn from the ground
resisting banshee gales.

They lost what little hold
tied them to shelves of stone,
or snapped along their trunks
exposing russet hearts
of raw and splintered wood.

Long ribbons of shed bark
weave through upended bush,
lines of saplings spun
from earth and hope of growth.

Soon

her days will soften, sunlight
cleanse mildew from the path,
fingers lose the numbness
winter brings, nagging fissures
in bandaged thumbs can heal.
Secateurs will respond to pressure
and she can knot a cord again,
canes arching on the path tied back.

Soon
her face misted by retreating clouds
she will taste the scent of eucalypts
and mint bush swathed in flower,
see wattlebirds defend their patch
as banksia spikes unfold.
Today she is enclosed by walls
her thoughts are cold, they yearn
for sun and the quickening of spring.

Taken

The heavy sky warns of rain,
strong winds give voice
to downcast leaves, ask
where has the woman gone?

What misadventure in her mind,
misstep on snake or ledge,
when a daily walk to town
took unexpected twists?

She left no clues
to where her day was bound,
the gullies stretching deeper
as the weeks slip by.

Familiar paths can turn,
become an endless maze,
they mask our tracks
and hold their secrets well.

Our mystery-laden world, where
a woman walks in plain sight
of trees and ferns
but can't be found by man.

I am more

than timber you desire.
You shear me from the earth
and keep me in the shade,
no more to feel cicadas thrum,
the seasons' fall and growth.

No birds will sing or possums nest,
nor grubs feast on my leaves,
the generations who depend
on all I have to share
above and underground.

Saws reduce me to bald slabs,
a blank to stamp your name upon,
you rasp, chisel and you grind,
sand down the life I held
so you can see my heart.

Heritage

Elsewhere
streets are paved with history,
stories written in the walls.

Here we have
no sign posts to the past,
our learning comes from
reading stones and trees,
what flies or hops or climbs,
the silence in a mist
and battering of storms.

Escarpments crack
exposing naked rock
that weathers into grains.
We write on shadows
and footprints in the sand.

Spring

Wollemi

Within the blue horizon
where eucalypt oil distils,
ragged mountains hide
the relic of Jurassic time
waiting to be found.

In valleys masked by cloud
creeks pick and stumble
through escarpment falls,
a hiker enters history
and claims his dinosaur.

In city hulks of noise
and clammy haze
where mysteries are tamed,
the ancient pine is cloned,
adapts to life in pots,

kept as postmodern star
in high rent towers,
the feature on suburban blocks
of whip-edged turf,
far from its secret home.

Off Track

Led by a winding path
away from roads and lanes,
this filament through scrub
will lead me to the ridge.

The scent of nectar hangs
in pale translucent flowers,
with acid shots of tangerine
where fungi swells on wood.

I reach a cambered ledge
as ground gives way to sky,
my path dissolves in cloud
I lack the wings to tread.

Hunger

At first glance
the garden swells with growth,
pale translucent leaves unfurl
until my view is closed,
all I see is green on green.

Come close, observe –
grubs and snails and slugs,
spiders trap their world in silk.
The smallest leaf supports a host
of aphids, lerps and mites.

Birds pluck worms and moths,
caravans of ants – from buried nest
to highest bud trail up and down all day.
A bite sized harvest, piece by piece,
the garden fills with mouths.

Ringtail

A trail of branch ends on the path
leads towards her nest, a knot
of leaves that I can almost touch.

When the garden closes into night
and we are locked inside the house,
she wakes, softly comes to feed.

Tonight with torch and quiet steps
I find her couched above my head
deep in the plum's spring growth.

She is smaller than a cat, is shy
but does not leave, to one side
her miniature watches how I move.

Small enough to cradle in my palm,
a wide-eyed stare that has no fear,
it learns torches don't have teeth.

Natural Light

Above the noise of birds
our garden thrums with bees.
Somewhere unknown
a hive grows plump
until it's overwhelmed.

One half takes flight,
brings its dark mass
to weigh the branches down
beside our orchard path.
We watch enthralled

safe behind our glass,
wild bees have chosen us
to build their home beside.
Our glowing rooms
extend their working hours.

Next morning when we rise
the swarm has flown,
they do not wish to share
in our unnatural days,
to base their lives around
our artificial sun.

Until today

I never held a snake,
presumed it was repellent,
rasping scales above
an earthworm clammy
feel upon my skin,

that I would panic
as it slithered upward,
tongue flickering my scent,
arabesqued
to curl around my neck.

Instead his touch is firm,
sensuous and smooth,
warmed by the sun
he is delicate but strong.
Close to my nose

I admire the intricate
mosaic of his scales,
assured no harm will come
as we look heart to eye,
trusting this is true.
I hope we can be friends.

How to Make a Home

By daily bending to the earth,
the alchemy of time and craft,
learning how to read the land
turns ragged soil into a nest.

Where apples spread unruly limbs
as pear trees rise towards the clouds
peaches, plums and figs entwine,
an orchard bound with twisting paths
and untamed thatch above.

Winter's drought, dry banks and trunks
becomes spring's flood of growth,
blossom, seeds, emerging fruit
that never ripen on the stem.

With parent guides, fledglings come,
learn how to eat and master flight,
unsteady hops from branch to branch
till they can soar, glide and swoop.
Wings are the heartbeats of my home.

The Bowerbird

Sheltered by a thatch of leaves
the young male tends a mound,
his busy back and forth
beneath the limbs of plum,
days lengthen, swell to bud,

around a frame of waratah
he gathers spent wisteria stems,
builds a floor and walls,
the stage where he can dance,
females preen, drawn to his bower,

he directs their gaze
with broken pegs and bottle lids,
berries of the blueberry ash,
strips from a fretted tarp,
appealing to his audience

he gives a warbling trill cascade
that changes to staccato rounds,
head down, wings out
he pirouettes with complex moves,
an older male is unimpressed,

next day reveals the raid,
walls crushed, his stage disbursed
and nothing blue remains,
while females build their nests
his rival guards its plundered trove.

The Colony

The young came early
teased into life by warming air,
suckled, drowsed, began to grow,
cushioned on discordant noise,
held beneath their mothers' wings,
dark fruit inhabiting the forest's edge.
Trees protect the colony with shade
above moist quilts of falling leaves.

Moonlit silhouettes,
a silent grace in flight,
the fruit bats feast, return
and jostle for a perch to sleep.
Each night sharp claws shred leaves,
strip the roost back to raw limbs
stark against the morning light.

Another day of desiccating winds,
heat rising from the ground below,
exposed, without a sheltering canopy,
asleep and trapped they cannot breathe
cling-wrapped in folded wings.
The colony falls like ripened pears
with babies on their teats.

The Work of Noise

A canopy of rough barked trees
gives shelter from the storms,
a woodland dense with life,
the seasonal exchange
wrapped in a world of leaves.

Old growth with history of fires
and rot makes nesting sites,
a place for young
to lift their wings in flight,
land softly on the scrub.

We wake to grader throb,
the grunt and grind of shifting rock,
chainsaw drone and falling trees,
a constant beat of heavy trucks
eclipse the days of spring.

Gums transform to woodchip pyres,
a road with concrete edge and drains
grows from levelled earth,
fresh bitumen dries in the sun
and from it silence flows.

Plovers in the Park

On a patch of dirt between two vans
she makes her nest, squawks in alarm
when we come near, rising on her stilts
defends three blue-green speckled eggs.

Old campers know her well,
protect her plot with flags and sticks,
alert to nosey dogs and shunting rigs,
men with tents on flat bed trucks.

She blasts them all with piercing cries,
her mate swoops at their heads.
Hatchlings learn to mimic stones,
with luck they'll find the sky.

The Watchers

The Chinese elms
keep their branches low,
leaves saw-toothed and fine
spread green clouds beneath
a jag-edged urban sky.

Jacarandas defy neat lawns,
shed drifts of violet haze,
thrust gangly limbs
light-headed to the sun
scattering their leaves.

The stately masts of gums,
sharp scent of citrus oil
rising from crushed leaves
blends with mown grass
and bursts of petrol fumes.

Trees bend to change and wind,
hold the sandstone heights,
they watch the harbour work,
in groups or on their own
the trees command it all.

Shearwater

Above the pulsing waves
an island outcrop soars,
its craggy, knotted rocks
engulfed by nesting birds,
each burrow marked with cries.

A mother has returned
disgorging all she holds,
her downy, trembling chick
in constant, squawking need.

Each day he's left exposed
to gulls and beating storms.

She seeks the choicest food
among the gleaming shoals,
her chick is ripe to fledge
but then he slowly fades.

When rangers find the chick,
mere feathers glued to bone,
his belly still contains
the knot of plastic shapes
a mother thought were fish.

Fire Ready

The saplings' russet leaves,
geebung fruit, waratahs
and banksias in full bloom
crushed beneath
a tractor's scoop and blade.

Home to native bees
and nectar seeking birds,
the undergrowth is cleared,
a fire break, ready for
the danger summer brings.

A scent of eucalypts
hanging in the air
long after trees have gone.

Fire Healing

Grey mists
are rising through the pines,
past apple trees' dense shade,
fruit spread upon the ground.

We gather in a timbered room,
hug shawls against
the chill November day.

We're here to grieve,
express what each has known
when shearing winds
brought fire into our lives,

took all we owned
or left us seared
by flames we'd known before,

learnt how emotions
hold the body's reins,
and tears need space
to fall upon new ground.

Outside is soaking rain.

Devotional

I raise my eyes
towards red domes,
not some cathedral town
or faded Byzantine,
I see arching stems of waratah,
bracts nectar-filled, packed tight,
topped by gilded terminals.

Here are bronzes to revere,
eucalypts' young leaves,
these sculptures glow
with morning light,
ephemeral as my hours.
Each one sustains me
as a song of praise.

www.ingramcontent.com/pod-product-compliance
Lightning Source LLC
Chambersburg PA
CBHW062151100526
44589CB00014B/1780